Your Amazing Itty Bitty® Staying Young at Any Age Book

15 Simple Steps to Extreme Anti-Aging

50 is the new 30, 60 is the new 40, 70 is the new 50, and yes -- 80 is the new 60!

In this cutting edge Itty Bitty Book, Dianna Whitley shows you simple, fast techniques to look and feel young again. Dianna feels better and has more energy now than she did when she was 40 – using the steps in this book.

Follow these 15 simple butt important steps, and you'll be astonished at how youthful you will become. For example:

- Breathing methods that create instant energy
- 6 stress busters that really work
- Ingredients in products for younger skin
- Exercising less and benefiting more
- Spices and oils that reverse the aging process
- The 3 major enemies of staying young

Most importantly–these tips work!

Pick up a copy of this powerful book today so you can look and feel younger than you ever thought possible.

Reviews

Dianna Whitley's "Staying Young at Any Age Book" is full of practical, common sense and FUN ways to get and maintain a youthful life! It is remarkably comprehensive for being an Itty Bitty Book and a great reference to keep on the coffee table or carry with you. Pick it up once or twice a day and turn to any page for helpful tips and reminders of how to stay young! Judging by the way Dianna looks, the information she shares in her book really works!!!
    Rev. Jenny Dickason, Phoenix, AZ

I loved this Book! A lot of research went into it, I'm sure. Very well written and I appreciate the sense of humor too. There is a whole lot of information packed into this Itty Bitty Book and it is information that I need to remember. Thank you so much!
    Carole Tru Foster

This quick read summarizes everything we need to do to feel good every day! It is a hand guide I can keep in my purse, on my desk, or next to my bed to remind myself every day.
    Claire Romero

Your Amazing Itty Bitty® Staying Young At Any Age Book

*15 Simple Steps
To Turn Back the Clock*

Dianna Whitley

Published by Itty Bitty® Publishing
A subsidiary of S & P Productions, Inc.

Copyright © 2016 Dianna Whitley

All rights reserved. No part of this book may be reproduced or transmitted in any form or by any means, electronic or mechanical, including photocopying, recording or by any information storage and retrieval system, without written permission of the publisher, except for inclusion of brief quotations in a review.

Printed in the United States of America

Itty Bitty® Publishing
311 Main Street, Suite D
El Segundo, CA 90245
(310) 640-8885

ISBN: 978-1-931191-00-5

This book is dedicated with many thanks to Suzy Prudden, Joan Meijer, and Suzanne Munshower, who have been getting younger along with me.

Stop by our Itty Bitty® website to find interesting blog entries about staying young at any age!

www.IttyBittyPublishing.com

And for ongoing tips and details on ways to look and feel great no matter how old you are, go to:

www.StayingYoungAtAnyAge.com

Table of Contents

	Introduction
Step 1.	Think and Grow Young
Step 2.	Get Younger While You Breathe
Step 3.	Younger Skin
Step 4	Know Your Enemies: Inflammation
Step 5.	Staying Young with Essential Oils
Step 6.	Know Your Enemies: Stress
Step 7.	Younger Energy
Step 8.	Reel Back the Years While You Sleep
Step 9.	Know Your Enemies: Sugar
Step 10.	Eat and Age Backwards
Step 11.	Staying Young with Exercise
Step 12.	Drink from the Fountain of Youth
Step 13.	The Mane Thing: Younger Hair
Step 14	Act Young, Feel Young, Get Young
Step 15.	The Top 20 Ways to Look & Feel Old

Introduction

"If I'd known I was going to live this long I would have taken better care of myself."
~ Peter O'Toole

This book will give you great tips on looking and feeling far younger than you really are, no matter what you've done–or not done–in the past. It's not magic. The aging process is real, but it can be slowed down enormously, and aspects of it can even be reversed.

After all, 60 is the new 40, 70 is the new 50, and 80 is the new 60. So let's get started!

Step 1
Think and Grow Young

Everything starts in the mind–especially looking and feeling younger. Keep your mind young, and your body will follow. The Mind-Body connection is real!

Pick out role models from TV, movies, and your own friends and acquaintances. Look at them from the aspect of how youthful they seem, and adopt the characteristics that you admire.

1. Tell people how old you are, enjoy the look of surprise on their faces –and bask in the warmth of hearing how good you look.
2. Attitude really is everything.
3. Go back in time: what did you really love to do when you were a kid? Paint? Draw? Write? Help people? Play the saxophone? Travel to exotic places? Notice what makes you feel good, and do more of that, every day. Dance! Sing! Even if it's just in your own living room!

Good Role Models

Celebrity role models:

- Patti LaBelle, 70
- Diana Ross, 70
- Barbra Streisand, 73
- Tina Turner, 74
- Al Pacino, 76
- Justice Ruth Bader Ginsburg, 82
- Halle Berry, 50
- Gloria Steinem, 82
- Diane Keaton, 70
- Sean Connery, 86

According to people interviewed in *People Magazine*, some secrets to staying young include:

- Jane Fonda (79) says to let go of perfectionism.
- Judi Dench (81) recommends never retiring.
- Clint Eastwood (85) believes in meditation and a good diet.
- Raquel Welch (75) does yoga.

Note: The ages listed above are as of the publication of this book in 2015.

Step 2
Get Younger While You Breathe

We can live 3 weeks without eating, and 3 days without water, but we can only live about 3 or 4 minutes without breathing–and yet, most people don't breathe well at all.

Few other things can give you more energy, help you sleep better at night, make you look and feel years younger, and improve your health!

1. Breathe from your stomach. Take a moment and put your hand there. If it moves in and out when you breathe, you're doing it right. If your shoulders move up and down, you're breathing from your chest, and not getting enough oxygen.
2. Set a timer and check your breathing once an hour. Since most of us have smartphones, that should be easy to do. When it goes off, focus on your breath. If you're like 99% of the western world, you need to BREATHE!

Tense or In Pain?

These techniques work like magic even though they're so simple it's hard to believe they really work. However, I have taught them to literally thousands of people, with great success!

- Take a deep breath, and count to 10. Exhale. Repeat 10 times. Slow your breathing down each time if until you get to 10. If you can't get that far, that's OK– count to 4 or 5. You'll get there over time. Even if you have intense pain, this works.

- Still in pain? I call this technique "Breathing in a Box," and it's nothing short of miraculous. To do it, breathe in 4 equal parts. Breathe in to the count of 5, hold the air in to the count of 5, breathe out to the count of 5, and do not breathe in again for the count of 5. The last step is the most important part. As well as using it for pain, it also is effective for getting centered and stress reduction.

For more tips on powerful ways to increase your energy, relax, and feel better with powerful breathing techniques go to:
www.StayingYoungAtAnyAge.com

Step 3
Younger Skin

Your skin is your largest organ. You can't totally eliminate the ravages of age, but there are things you can do to retain that youthful glow.

1. Drink more water, sleep 7-8 hours a night, and exercise.
2. Eat well, and include fat in your diet. Your skin needs it. So does your brain and your heart. Without those organs, what difference does your skin make?
3. Wild salmon is full of nutrients such as the omega-3s that keep the skin nice and plump, and protein, which is critical.
4. Sunglasses protect the delicate skin around the eyes and keep you from squinting, which can create more wrinkles.
5. Use a good moisturizer, preferably with hyaluronic acid, which binds water to and plumps up the skin. Use a lip balm with a full spectrum sunscreen.
6. Hands and elbows are especially susceptible the aging process. Use creams that have vitamin C, shea butter, or coconut oil, and a lightening agent to fade age spots.

Younger on the Outside

- Use a broad spectrum sunscreen even when it's cloudy, and refresh it every 4 hours. Don't think you need it? Just take a look at the skin on your stomach–it's probably as flawless as a baby's.
- Melanoma is a sure-fire way to stop the aging process altogether. It is the one cancer that's completely curable if detected early, and almost totally incurable if it isn't. Notice something unusual? See your doctor. I've had three, and NOT ONE of them looked like the pictures you see in books.
- Exfoliate to get rid of dead, dry skin and let the fresher skin underneath come up, but be gentle, or you may damage the skin. Alpha hydroxy acids (AHAs) are also good for exfoliating.
- Retinol stimulates collagen, which fights wrinkles. Over the counter (OTC) isn't as good as the prescription Retinoid, but much less expensive. *But,* be meticulous about sunscreen, as your skin will be more sensitive to sun damage!
- Use only 1 or 2 new anti-aging products at a time, so you don't irritate your skin.
- Sleep on your back, instead of your side or your stomach!

Step 4
Know Your Enemies: Inflammation

Research confirms that chronic inflammation is a major cause of almost every disease and health condition.

1. Don't smoke: it hardens the arteries. You can reverse all the damage by quitting.
2. Eat Mediterranean: fish, fruits and vegetables, whole grains, nuts, and olives.
3. Get active. Not too much and not too little. Exercise for 30 to 45 minutes, 5 days a week, swimming, bicycling, or brisk walking.
4. Shrink your waist size. If you're a woman with more than 35 inches or a man with more than 40 inches, you probably have a lot of inflammation.
5. Get enough sleep. Not too much (more than 8 hours), not too little (less than 6).
6. Reduce stress. Spend 15 minutes a day relaxing with deep breathing, meditation, music, reading, or a bubble bath.
7. Don't drink more than 2 alcoholic drinks a day. More can damage the intestinal lining and let bacteria into the bloodstream, causing inflammation.

Good News/Bad News

- Just a few hours of sitting decreases your HDL the good cholesterol, impedes your ability to remove fats and toxins, and turns off the "power" to the skeletal muscles (because we operate on something just like electricity). The result? Inflammation, and all its nasty by-products.
- Several major studies have confirmed that prolonged sitting is as severe a risk to your health as smoking–especially for cancer and cardiovascular disease. And it doesn't matter whether you exercise regularly or not!
- There is a solution, and it is astonishingly simple. Get up and walk around every half hour for just 1–5 minutes! It improves your glucose metabolism, keeps your skeletal muscles switched on, and lowers the risk of diabetes, cancer, and cardiovascular disease.
- As easy it sounds to do the above, it can actually be quite challenging, but only for while. When I began, I set the timer on my phone. At first I couldn't believe how fast it went off, or how irritating it was to stop what I was doing, but it got easier as I reminded myself of the benefits– and the dire consequences if I didn't do it!

Step 5
Staying Young with Essential Oils

Essential oils are extracted from plants and have been used for centuries for therapeutic purposes. Because your sense of smell is closely connected to stress-response and emotional centers of the brain, they can have a powerful effect on your mood and your general health.

1. Clove oil was used for hundreds of years in dentistry as an antiseptic and local anesthetic.
2. 1937 a French chemist discovered the healing properties of essential oils when he burned his hand and accidentally plunged it into a vat of pure lavender oil, thinking it was water.
3. In WWII Dr. Valnet used lavender oil to treat the injuries of wounded soldiers.
4. As always, with anything that can be therapeutic, check with your doctor–especially if you are pregnant or have a specific medical condition.
5. My personal favorites: Lavender, Peppermint, Orange, Frankincense, and Lemon Oil.

Simple Ways to Use Essential Oils

- Lavender oil is very relaxing and is often used to help with insomnia. It is also good for burns and cuts.
- Add 1-2 drops of peppermint to a glass of water. It's good for the digestion, it will give you energy–and it's delicious! Make sure it's organic, pure, and therapeutic grade however.
- Put 5-7 drops of lemon oil in a small spray bottle, with water and castile soap, to clean countertops and floors. Your home will smell wonderful.
- Orange oil shows anxiety-reducing effects when compared with a control.
- Frankincense was called "liquid gold" in ancient times and is very effective for pain, skin conditions, and inflammation.
- Apply oils to your palms, soles of your feet, or temples.

For more information on oils and their uses, go to www.StayingYoungAtAnyAge.com or www.LifeIsWonderful.com

Step 6
Know Your Enemies: Stress

Our fast paced world brings us the worst type of stress; the kind that can be unnoticed but deadly. It's called "Super-Stress" and it can actually change the structure of the cells in your brain, lead to panic attacks, phobias, high blood pressure, chemical dependency, eating disorders, and even a heart attack or stroke.

Here's a list that should get your attention: Stress has been directly linked to:

1. Diabetes and pre-diabetes
2. Accelerated aging
3. High blood pressure, heart disease, and stroke
4. A compromised immune system
5. Gastrointestinal issues like acid reflux
6. Obesity
7. Addictions
8. Anxiety and depression
9. Chronic insomnia
10. Memory loss

Stress Busters

The kind of stress that you feel before making a speech or doing something demanding is normal. If you think of it as excitement instead of stress, it will have a whole different feeling and impact.

- Meditation has been proven to be one of the best antidotes to stress on the planet.

* Laughing or spending time with friends is a huge combatant against stress.

* Hypnosis is a powerful and easy way to relax. For a selection of audios go to: www.StayingYoungAtAnyAge.com

* Pets are more than just a major source of happiness – they have actually been proven to reduce the physical and emotional ravages of stress.

* "Always look at the Bright Side of Life!" ~ Monty Python

* Acupuncture can significantly alleviate stress and its damaging outcomes.

- If you're stressed out about friends or relatives, it might help to remember that they are probably as stressed about you, and feel equally justified! (paraphrased from Wayne Dyer)

Step 7
Younger Energy

You can have more energy than you ever thought possible! One simple way to do that is to boost your metabolism. Our bodies are like wood burning stoves that need to be constantly stoked. Here are some ways:

1. Eat more! This might surprise you, but many people don't eat enough. Most women need about 1,200 calories, or their metabolism goes down. You need to eat enough to fuel your body's basic functions.
2. Eat often. About every 3 to 4 hours, to keep your metabolism burning.
3. Eat organic. Researchers found that people with a lot of pollutants from pesticides (stored in fat cells), have lower metabolism, possibly because the toxins interfere with the energy-burning process. This is especially important with most fruits, so eat organic whenever you can.
4. Eat fresh food, not processed
5. Eat simple, plant-based foods as often as possible.

High Energy Foods

- Eggs are one of earth's perfect foods, as they contain all 9 of the essential amino acids your body needs. Studies show that eating a protein-rich breakfast lessens hunger and provides energy throughout the day. The high protein in eggs makes them a great choice.
- Chia seeds are full of healthy anti-inflammatory fats, and a tablespoon has a walloping 2,500 mgs of omega-3 fatty acids, 4.5 grams of fiber, 3 grams of protein, and tons of phytonutrients.
- Green tea, black tea, and coffee activate the sympathetic nervous system. Green tea acts as a prebiotic, supporting the growth of fat-burning friendly flora. Coffee can raise your metabolism 5 to 8%, and surprisingly, a cup of black tea can raise your metabolism by 12% because of the antioxidant catechins in it.
- Green foods like chorella, spirulina, barley grass, and wheatgrass promote energy and optimum health. The easiest way to eat them is in a smoothie.
- Cinnamon has been proven to help block the absorption of glucose, and stabilize blood sugar. Add it to your coffee or tea and enjoy its fat-burning properties.

Step 8
Reel Back the Years While You Sleep

Getting enough good, solid sleep is an important key to staying young and full of energy–and the opposite is also true. Not enough, too much, or bad sleep insures early aging!

- Getting 5 hours or less of sleep increases blood pressure and inflammation.
- People who get 7 to 8 hours of quality sleep have slimmer waistlines – a basic indicator of overall health.
- An NIH study showed that adults who get at least seven hours of sleep per night tend to have up to 20 years less damage and deterioration on a cellular level.
- Brain scans prove that people who sleep well crave less food because they create more of the hormone leptin, which suppresses the appetite.
- Eat your last meal 3 hours before you go to sleep. If you do want to eat something right before bed, protein is your best bet.
- Take 30–60 minutes to unwind before you go to bed. Listen to music, read a book. (Did you notice that the TV and computer are NOT on this list?)

Sleep, Glorious Sleep Aids

- Valerian, melatonin, and lavender oil are potent enhancers of good sleep.
- Listen to a relaxation audio (go to www.StayingYoungAtAnyAge.com)
- Limit any nap to 30 minutes, and take it by mid-day.
- Take time before you go to bed to unwind with a book or hot bath. Listening to relaxation audios, self-hypnosis or calming music also helps.
- Your brain interprets the light from TV and computer screens as full daylight. Being online or watching television right before going to bed will make it harder to fall asleep.
- We're creatures of habit. Your mind and your body respond well to consistency. Have a schedule, and change it as little as possible.
- If you're hungry, eat protein. It contains L-tryptophan, the amino acid that helps produce melatonin.
- If you get up in the middle of the night use a flashlight or night-light for illumination. Bright light sends a signal to the brain that it's time to wake up.

Step 9
Know Your Enemies: Sugar

Until 100 years ago, sugar was something only the wealthy could afford. Now it's become one of our biggest health risks, causing high insulin levels that can lead to premature aging, high blood pressure and cholesterol, heart disease, diabetes, and obesity.

1. Today, our diets are saturated with sugar and high fructose corn syrup (HFCS). A Harvard study showed that just one sweet drink a day created an 83% higher risk of type 2 diabetes.
2. Dr. John Yudkin, MD of the University of London found that people with cardiovascular disease ate twice as much sugar on average as people without, and that sugar was far more to blame for obesity and heart disease than either fat or cholesterol.
3. In 1893 there were less than 3 cases of diabetes per 100.000 people in the US. There are 29.1 million diabetics today. That's almost 8000 per 100,000 people. 90% of them have type 2.

The Sugar Scoop

In 2009, the American Heart Association advised adults to eat no more than 6 teaspoons of added sugars a day for women, and 9 teaspoons for men (based on average weight).

- Do the numbers. Since 4 grams equals 1 teaspoon, you can calculate the number of teaspoons by dividing the number of grams by 4. For example, 24 grams = 6 teaspoons. and 36 grams = 9 teaspoons.
- "Nonfat" food usually means there is more sugar in it than if it *did* have fat – because if it didn't, it would taste like cardboard.
- 27% of the US population now has "Metabolic Syndrome," or Insulin Resistance, the precursors to type-2 diabetes.
- Some foods with hidden sugar:
Spaghetti sauce (1 cup) 23 grams
Barbecue sauce (1/2 cup) 33 grams
Fat-free fruit yogurt (1 cup) 47 grams
Bottled ice tea (1 cup) 22 grams

For Tips on Kicking the Sugar Habit, go to:
www.StayingYoungAtAnyAge.com

Step 10
Eat and Age Backwards

Diets don't work unless you stay on them. And who wants to do that? Some people swear by the Paleo Diet, Vegetarianism, the Zone, but I like to keep things simple.

1. Enjoy what you eat. Stressing out over your food will be worse for you than almost anything you eat (not including the obvious culprits).
2. Eat as few processed foods as possible. Period.
3. Grains are good, when they are whole: brown rice, whole wheat pasta, popcorn (very lightly salted, and with olive oil instead of butter), and the magical ancient grains: quinoa, amaranth, faro, spelt and kamut.
4. Make your individual portion sizes about the size of a woman's fist.
5. Nourish yourself with nuts. They're rich in omega-3 fatty acids. Just not too many! A quarter cup at the most.

Eat Your Way to Being Younger

- Read labels. If you can't pronounce a lot of the ingredients, don't eat it, or eat as little and infrequently as possible
- Avoid MSG.
- If you eat processed foods, they are high in salt and sugar. Research recommends about 1500 mg of sodium and no more 6 teaspoons (24 grams) of sugar a day. Assume you will eat 5 grams before you even start counting.
- Eat protein, healthy fat and fiber together to slow down the digestion process.
- Avocado is packed with nutrients! Eating them once a day keeps the doctor away.
- Nuts are good for you – just not too many
- Have a blender drink almost every day. With a whey or vegetarian protein, powdered vegetables, and Chia seeds. Because there is lot to be said for chewing. eat something small and low calorie at the same time.

Recipes for delicious, nutritious meals, smoothies, and snacks can be found at:

www.StayingYoungAtAnyAge.com

Step 11
Staying Young with Exercise.

Yes, you need to do it. When you think about exercise, "you can lie down till the thought passes," (per Woody Allen) or you can just do it!

1. Walk at least 30 minutes a day, at least 3 times a week. Studies prove that walking is as good for your heart and health as jogging. And better for your knees!
2. Get a dog – or volunteer to walk dogs at your local shelter.
3. Sex drive low? Exercise isn't just good for your body – it's good for your brain, and your brain is your biggest sex organ!
4. Put exercise on your schedule. And when you stick to it, reward yourself once a week with something you really want, whether it's going to a movie or meeting a friend for lunch. Better yet – take a walk with them instead!
5. Need some more motivation? Is your memory starting to get fuzzy? Exercise brings blood and oxygen to your brain. It will clear out the cobwebs.
6. It might sound obvious – but when you exercise, breathe deeply, keep a good posture, and let yourself enjoy it!

Exercise Before You Get Out Of Bed

- Great bed exercises include:
    - Leg crosses
    - Pelvic tilts
    - Bicycling on your back
    - Clams
    - Leg Scissors
    - Child Pose
    - Cobra
    - Ankle Circles

Most of these are commonly known, or you can get step-by-step directions at:

www.StayingYoungAtAnyAge.com

- Exercise throughout the day. Park as far away from your destinations as you can, use the stairs instead of the elevator, sprint instead of walking, do stomach "pulls" and Kegels while you're waiting in line, and stretch all through the day.
- Have more sex. It's great exercise!
- You know this, but I will say it anyway. Exercise increases your circulation, promotes good sleep, and helps keep your brain as well as your body healthy.

Step 12
Drink from the Fountain of Youth

The 3 basic foundations of life are food, air, and water. Our planet wouldn't be habitable without water, and neither are our bodies.

1. One of the prime enemies to youthfulness is dehydration, whether it is in your skin, your hair, or your internal organs.
2. Signs you are dehydrated: Fatigue, muscle cramps, constipation, and dark yellow urine (it should be clear or light yellow).
3. Acid of any kind is not your friend, and water is one of the most basic ways to stay alkaline. Many doctors and health practitioners believe this is the most fundamental rule to good health.
4. Rule of thumb: If you feel very thirsty, you are already dehydrated.
5. Dehydration isn't just an enemy of youthfulness, it is a health risk. A friend did a cleanse without enough water, and ended up in the hospital for 3 days!
6. There are entire books written about how drinking enough clean, filtered water affects every aspect of your health.

Water, Water, Everywhere.

- You need to drink approximately one ounce of water for every 2 pounds of body weight. (60 ounces for a 120 pounds), or 8 to 10 glasses a day.
- Fill up the amount you decide on in a pitcher – or separate bottles – every morning, and make sure you have drunk all of it by the end of the day.
- Set a timer on your smart phone and drink a set amount every half hour to an hour.
- Finish drinking most of your water intake within 2 hours of going to bed, so you will be less likely to wake up in the middle of the night.
- Test your skin or hydration by pinching the top of your hand. If it takes more than 5 - 10 seconds to flatten, you are dehydrated.
- There is controversy whether all your water needs to come from just water, or whether some of it can come from water rich vegetables and fruits, and herbal teas. Try both approaches, and see how your skin reacts.

Step 13
The Mane Thing: Younger Hair

More than any other change you can make to your look, having a good hairstyle with the right color and length for you is one of the biggest secrets to looking younger. Here are some tips:

1. Make a file of pictures from magazines that you think would look good on you.
2. Take selfies, with your phone, camera, or computer. Make a file on your computer so you have them in one place. Look at them over time, and send a few to a good friend that will give you honest feedback.
3. Seek out a good hairstylist. That doesn't mean the most expensive one in town – just a good one, who will work with you, and teach you how to use the right products and tools at home.
4. Try new looks. Experiment. The thing about hair is that no matter how badly one of your experiments might turn out, it will grow back!
5. Don't assume you need to dye your hair. Some women look stunning with white, gray, or silver hair, especially if they are comfortable with it. Just make sure your skin, makeup, and overall health are at their prime – or you will look old!

No More Bad Hair Days

- Use shampoo and conditioner containing Red Clover. Studies show this can make your hair 46% thicker in as little as 4 months, because it reduces the inflammation blocking new growth.
- Split ends make your hair look like a tumble weed. Use a glaze with silicone.
- Your Mother was right – brushing your hair 100 times a day is good for it. But if that's too much- try 30!
- Fighting the frizzies? Skim your hair with a little hair cream (you can even use hand cream), and clip it into a twist for about 10 minutes. When you unclip it, you will be amazed at how much smoother it looks!
- Bend over for a boost in hair growth. Reach for your toes, or sit with your head between your knees. Minakshi Welukar, MD says doing this for 4 minutes a day can increase blood flow to the scalp, adding more nutrients and oxygen, and causing your hair to grow more within weeks!
- Highlights around the face make a person look younger.

Step 14
Act Young, Feel Young, Get Young

What did you want to do when you were a kid? Do those things now!

1. Travel – especially to foreign countries. We take so much for granted, and it will put things into perspective. It's a great way to meet interesting people – the ones who live in the places you visit, as well as your fellow travelers.
2. Be grateful. This has been proven to work on a chemical level. Gratitude and the feeling of appreciation stimulate the brain to create dopamine and its first cousin, serotonin.
3. Touching is very powerful. It boosts the immune system and creates a sense of well-being and happiness. A simple hug releases oxytocin in the brain, so hug as long and as often as you can. And treat yourself to massages.
4. Find something you're passionate about and commit yourself to doing it.
5. Get a pet. (You will see this tip on several of these pages.)
6. Laugh. Long and often, every day.

Just Do It!

- Don't hold back how you feel and what you think. I don't mean that you should be mean or rude – but speak up. Say what you mean. It's one of the joys of being older!
- Stop worrying. It doesn't change a thing. Make a decision. You can always change it, but in the meantime, you have gotten out of the quagmire of negative energy, and into action, which increases the dopamine in your brain.
- Express yourself. Paint, play music, be involved in a play, write, dance…
- Adopt a dog or cat from an animal shelter.
- Eliminate perfectionism. It's a major destroyer of good things.
- Spend time with younger people. They tend to be more fun, and you will get more energized by osmosis.
- Volunteer. Be a Big Brother or Big Sister, help a good cause, or a homeless or animal shelter. Here's a secret worth knowing – you're the one who will benefit the most.

Step 15
The Top 20 Ways to Look and Feel Old

1. Eat lots of sugar, salt, & processed foods.
2. Sleep less than 7 hours a night.
3. Watch a lot of TV.
4. Keep your house too warm in the winter.
5. Use a straw when you drink. It's great for creating wrinkles.
6. Smoke. Even just a few a day will do.
7. Be inactive, and in particular, sit a lot.
8. Worry and get stressed out about things.
9. Complain as often as possible.
10. Don't use the handrail on stairs.
11. Don't wear sunscreen.
12. Be rigid and insist on having things your way.
13. Talk about how much better things were "in the good old days."
14. Mention every little ache and pain.
15. Don't watch where you're walking.
16. Go out as little as possible.
17. Don't eat your vegetables.
18. Be at least 30 pounds overweight.
19. Slouch, and shuffle your feet.
20. Don't floss.

A Few Last Tips

- Drink a glass of water when you wake up - you just went through 8 hours of dehydration! Better yet, add a little lemon, or lemon oil.
- Entire books have been written about apple cider vinegar. 2 tablespoons in a glass of water can alleviate an upset stomach, and it's good for leg cramps at night because it has a lot of potassium. Sore throat? Gargle with 2 oz. of apple cider vinegar and an equal amount of warm water.
- To stay young, one of the best things you can do is to be at your ideal weight. Want some powerful help with that? Go to Your Amazing Itty Bitty® Weight Loss Book by Suzy Prudden and Joan Meijer.
- Green Foods are also a major antidote to low energy and a host of health issues. Broccoli, barley, sprouts, cabbage, squash, collards, beans, peppers, kale, and asparagus are all golden, not just green!

You've finished. Before you go…

Please star rate this book.

Reviews are solid gold to writers. Please take a few minutes to give us some itty bitty feedback on this book. Many thanks.

ABOUT THE AUTHOR

Dianna Whitley is a writer and photographer, as well as a Certified Hypnotherapist and Life Coach. Her work has been published in over 60 countries, and includes the book *Beauty on the Go (*Simon & Schuster*)* with Jackie Zeman of General Hospital.

She has photographed TV and movie stars such as Marie Osmond, Patrick Dempsey, Grace Jones, Ann-Margaret, John Stamos, Burt Reynolds, Elizabeth Taylor, Michael J. Fox, Demi Moore, David Hasselhoff, Mario Lopez, and many others. Her photos have appeared in The New York Times, People Magazine, Us Weekly, and TV Guide.

She also owned three hypnosis centers in California, where she and her staff helped over 7000 people reach their weight loss and health goals.

Dianna grew up in Connecticut, and has lived in NYC, Boston, Vermont, the Bahamas, Puerto Rico, Santa Fe, and Phoenix. Dianna currently lives in Las Vegas – but she tells friends and relatives to always put her address in pencil.

www.StayingYoungAtAnyAge.com

**If You Enjoyed This Book
You Might Also Enjoy**

- **Your Amazing Itty Bitty® Weight Loss Book** – Suzy Prudden and Joan Meijer-Hirschland

- **Your Amazing Itty Bitty® Self-Esteem Book** – Jade Elizabeth

- **Your Amazing Itty Bitty® Gratitude Book** – Belinda Lee Cook

And our many other Itty Bitty® Books are now available on line…

www.ingramcontent.com/pod-product-compliance
Lightning Source LLC
Chambersburg PA
CBHW061305040426
42444CB00010B/2520